BETH FLINTOFF

Beth is a playwright, dramaturg and theatre director. She is Associate Playwright and Young Writers Associate at the Royal Court Theatre in London.

Writing includes: *The Ballad of Maria Marten* (Eastern Angles); *The World We Made* (Warwick Arts Centre); *A Christmas Carol* (Reading Rep); *Henry I*, *Matilda the Empress*, *Henry II*, *Who Killed Alfred Oliver* and *The Last Abbot* (Rabble Theatre Company); *The Rivals* (Watermill Theatre); *The Glove Thief* (Tonic Platform Plays); *Milady* (commissioned for the Write the Girl project) and *Come to Where I'm From* (Paines Plough). She has collaborated twice as writer/director with physical-theatre ensemble Rhum and Clay, on *Jekyll and Hyde* and *Hardboiled: The Fall of Sam Shadow*. Beth also co-directed the multiple Off West End Award-winning play, *The Incident Room* with David Byrne for New Diorama.

For radio: *The Newcomers* and *Who Killed Alfred Oliver* (BBC Sounds/Rabble).

She was a member of the Sphinx Lab for British Female Playwrights 2020–2021 and a recipient of a 2021 MGCfutures Bursary. For *Rebellious Women* she received an Off West End Awards nomination for Best New Playwright in 2018. She is an Associate Artist at Rabble Theatre Company.

Other Titles in this Series

Ellen Brammar
MODEST

Chris Bush
THE ASSASSINATION OF KATIE HOPKINS
THE CHANGING ROOM
CHRIS BUSH PLAYS: ONE
A DOLL'S HOUSE *after* Ibsen
FAUSTUS: THAT DAMNED WOMAN
HUNGRY
JANE EYRE *after* Brontë
THE LAST NOËL
OTHERLAND
ROBIN HOOD AND THE
    CHRISTMAS HEIST
ROCK / PAPER / SCISSORS
STANDING AT THE SKY'S EDGE
    with Richard Hawley
STEEL

Jez Butterworth
THE FERRYMAN
THE HILLS OF CALIFORNIA
JERUSALEM
JEZ BUTTERWORTH PLAYS: ONE
JEZ BUTTERWORTH PLAYS: TWO
MOJO
THE NIGHT HERON
PARLOUR SONG
THE RIVER
THE WINTERLING

Caryl Churchill
BLUE HEART
CHURCHILL PLAYS: THREE
CHURCHILL PLAYS: FOUR
CHURCHILL PLAYS: FIVE
CHURCHILL: SHORTS
CLOUD NINE
DING DONG THE WICKED
A DREAM PLAY *after* Strindberg
DRUNK ENOUGH TO SAY I LOVE YOU?
ESCAPED ALONE
FAR AWAY
GLASS. KILL. BLUEBEARD'S FRIENDS.
    IMP.
HERE WE GO
HOTEL
ICECREAM
LIGHT SHINING IN BUCKINGHAMSHIRE
LOVE AND INFORMATION
MAD FOREST
A NUMBER
PIGS AND DOGS
SEVEN JEWISH CHILDREN
THE SKRIKER
THIS IS A CHAIR
THYESTES *after* Seneca
TRAPS
WHAT IF IF ONLY

Beth Flintoff
THE BALLAD OF MARIA MARTEN
THE GLOVE THIEF

James Fritz
COMMENT IS FREE & START SWIMMING
FALL
THE FLEA
LAVA
PARLIAMENT SQUARE
ROSS & RACHEL

Virginia Gay
CYRANO *after* Rostand

Lucy Kirkwood
BEAUTY AND THE BEAST
    with Katie Mitchell
BLOODY WIMMIN
THE CHILDREN
CHIMERICA
HEDDA *after* Ibsen
THE HUMAN BODY
IT FELT EMPTY WHEN THE HEART
    WENT AT FIRST BUT IT IS
    ALRIGHT NOW
LUCY KIRKWOOD PLAYS: ONE
MOSQUITOES
NSFW
RAPTURE
TINDERBOX
THE WELKIN

Maureen Lennon
HELEN
MARY AND THE HYENAS

Benedict Lombe
LAVA
SHIFTERS

Winsome Pinnock
LEAVE TAKING
PIG HEART BOY *after* Malorie Blackman
ROCKETS AND BLUE LIGHTS
TAKEN
TITUBA

Jessica Swale
BLUE STOCKINGS
THE JUNGLE BOOK *after* Rudyard Kipling
NELL GWYNN
THE PLAYHOUSE APPRENTICE

Jack Thorne
2ND MAY 1997
AFTER LIFE *after* Hirokazu Kore-eda
BUNNY
BURYING YOUR BROTHER IN
    THE PAVEMENT
A CHRISTMAS CAROL *after* Dickens
THE END OF HISTORY…
HOPE
JACK THORNE PLAYS: ONE
JACK THORNE PLAYS: TWO
JUNKYARD
LET THE RIGHT ONE IN
    after John Ajvide Lindqvist
THE MOTIVE AND THE CUE
MYDIDAE
THE SOLID LIFE OF SUGAR WATER
STACY & FANNY AND FAGGOT
WHEN WINSTON WENT TO WAR WITH
    THE WIRELESS
WHEN YOU CURE ME
WOYZECK *after* Büchner

debbie tucker green
BORN BAD
DEBBIE TUCKER GREEN PLAYS: ONE
DIRTY BUTTERFLY
EAR FOR EYE
HANG
NUT
A PROFOUNDLY AFFECTIONATE,
    PASSIONATE DEVOTION TO
    SOMEONE (– *NOUN*)
RANDOM
STONING MARY
TRADE & GENERATIONS
TRUTH AND RECONCILIATION

Beth Flintoff

REBELLIOUS WOMEN

NICK HERN BOOKS
London
www.nickhernbooks.co.uk

A Nick Hern Book

Rebellious Women first published in Great Britain as a paperback original in 2025 by Nick Hern Books Limited, The Glasshouse, 49a Goldhawk Road, London W12 8QP

Rebellious Women copyright © 2025 Beth Flintoff

Beth Flintoff has asserted her right to be identified as the author of this work

Front cover: photograph of Emma Denly in *Rebellious Women*, 2018, by Jon Holloway

Designed and typeset by Nick Hern Books, London
Printed in Great Britain by Mimeo Ltd, Huntingdon, Cambridgeshire PE29 6XX

A CIP catalogue record for this book is available from the British Library

ISBN 978 1 83904 437 3

CAUTION All rights whatsoever in this play are strictly reserved. Requests to reproduce the text in whole or in part should be addressed to the publisher.

Amateur Performing Rights Applications for performance, including readings and excerpts, by amateurs in the English language throughout the world should be addressed to the Performing Rights Department, Nick Hern Books, The Glasshouse, 49a Goldhawk Road, London W12 8QP, *tel* +44 (0)20 8749 4953, *email* rights@nickhernbooks.co.uk, except as follows:

Australia: ORiGiN Theatrical, Level 1, 213 Clarence Street, Sydney NSW 2000, *tel* +61 (2) 8514 5201, *email* enquiries@originmusic.com.au, *web* www.origintheatrical.com.au

New Zealand: Play Bureau, 20 Rua Street, Mangapapa, Gisborne, 4010, *tel* +64 21 258 3998, *email* info@playbureau.com

Professional Performing Rights Applications for performance by professionals in any medium and in any language throughout the world should be addressed in the first instance to Nick Hern Books, see details above.

No performance of any kind may be given unless a licence has been obtained. Applications should be made before rehearsals begin. Publication of this play does not necessarily indicate its availability for performance.

www.nickhernbooks.co.uk/environmental-policy

Nick Hern Books' authorised representative in the EU is
Easy Access System Europe – Mustamäe tee 50, 10621 Tallinn, Estonia
email gpsr.requests@easproject.com

This play was originally commissioned by Attic Theatre Company and first performed as *The Rebellious Women of Wimbledon* on 8 October 2018 at Merton Arts Space, Wimbledon Library. The cast was as follows:

EDITH	Emma Denly
ROSE	Valerie Antwi
BERTHA/GERVASE/TOM/EMILY	Ellen Attwell

All other parts were played by the company

Director	Jonathan Humphreys
Designer	Sarah Jane Booth
Sound Designer	Jon McLeod
Production Stage Manager	Lucy Myers
Fight Director	Yarit Dor
Executive Director (for Attic)	Victoria Hibbs

This version of *Rebellious Women* was commissioned and performed by St Albans High School for Girls on 7 March 2024. The cast was as follows:

EDITH	Kirsten Done
ROSE	Rosan Trisic
BERTHA	Shari Bassi
BEATRICE	Avery-Alex Hewitt
EMILY	Eleni Hadji-Savva
CONSTANCE	Holly White
GERVASE	Florence Z Dye
TOM	Margaux Hill
CHRISTABEL PANKHURST/ MRS GLADSTONE	Alice Withnell
WINSTON CHURCHILL/ PRISON GUARD	Katharine Thompson
DOCTOR/WALTER MCCLAREN	Darcey Foster
REV G. H. GODWIN/ SAMUEL BUTCHER	Tilly Pegg

Director	Holly Whymark
Production Manager	Alex Johnston
Costume and Props Supervisor	Emily Casimir-Brown
Sound Designer	Noah Angus
Video Designer	Robin Elwin
Production Coordinator	Anna Coxon
Front of House Coordinator	Zoë Briggs

Introduction
Beth Flintoff

Any child that grew up watching *Mary Poppins* knows that, once upon a time, well-to-do mothers wore sashes and sang songs in an enjoyably batty sort of way. But of course, the suffragette movement was so much more than that. When I started researching this play, I knew already that there was a darker side but hadn't fully grasped just how dark it was. These once-peaceful, law-abiding women were drawn into an increasingly subversive, dangerous world in which all existing structures, relationships, codes of conduct, ways in which men and women could coexist at all, had to be questioned. It must have felt like nothing would ever be the same again.

I became fascinated by the radicalisation of these young women. It's a shocking change in attitude for a conservative, conventional woman such as Edith to end up smashing a politician's window. I wanted to explore how it might be possible for someone as charismatic as Rose Lamartine Yates to draw others in, how they might bond together, urged on by faith, loyalty, friendship, and sisterly love. Once a suffragette had been imprisoned, they were often disowned by their families, so they had nobody else to turn to *except* the suffragettes. Society's disapproval did not make them change, it gave them no choice but to carry on.

This is a story about real people, but for the purposes of the drama I have condensed and juggled the timing of some of the events. For example, I have conflated Edith Begbie's two prison stays into one, to help speed the narrative along. Edith is, in fact, a compilation character – although there was an Edith Begbie who ran the WSPU shop, she did not have a husband called Gervase, and I have attributed some acts (such as vandalising the golf course) to Edith when in fact we don't know who did them. But I have tried, as faithfully as I can, to capture the essence of these women and the spirit of positive radicalism that seems to have been aflame in Wimbledon.

The first version of this play was called *The Rebellious Women of Wimbledon* and was created primarily to be performed in libraries and halls around South-West London, to celebrate the centenary of the first women being allowed the vote. Our cast of three performed in the round, with an audience on four sides, eating cake, occasionally joined by bemused book-browsers. Five years later I was delighted to be asked by Holly Whymark at St Albans High School for Girls if she could do it with a much larger cast. I enjoyed expanding the parts and including a tribute to the actions of Constance Bulwer-Lytton.

In conversation with friends recently I have been asking the question: if you were alive at this time, would you have been a law-breaking suffragette, a law-abiding suffragist, or neither? Most think they would have become a suffragist; some think they would have been a full-on suffragette; nobody thinks they'd have done nothing. I like to think I'd have been terrifically brave, but I wonder. To defy the structures of a system into which you have been born takes a courage I'm not sure I possess, despite enjoying the benefits. My overwhelming feeling now is one of gratitude to these women who trashed their own lives in order that someone like me can cast a vote. They are heroines, all of them.

Acknowledgements

I am incredibly grateful to Attic Theatre Company, especially Jonathan Humphreys for commissioning this story and providing such thoughtful dramaturgy. And then to Holly Whymark for her beautiful staging with a young and brilliant cast.

For support with research I am grateful to:

The family of Rose Lamartine Yates

The Women's Library at the London School of Economics

The John Innes Society

Peter Walker, Radical Walk Leader

Sarah Gould, Heritage & Local Studies Manager for Merton Council

Dr Alexandra Hughes Johnson

B.F.

Characters

THE SUFFRAGETTES
EDITH BEGBIE
ROSE LAMARTINE YATES
BERTHA LORSIGNOL
BEATRICE MONTGOMERY MARTIN
EMILY WILDING DAVISON
LADY CONSTANCE BULWER-LYTTON
CHRISTABEL PANKHURST

OTHER CHARACTERS
GERVASE BEGBIE, *Edith's husband*
TOM LAMARTINE YATES, *Rose's husband*
REVEREND G. H. GODWIN
WALTER McLAREN, *Member for Crewe*
SAMUEL BUTCHER, *Member for Cambridge*
WINSTON CHURCHILL, *Home Secretary*
MRS GLADSTONE SALOME ARDS, *Chairman of the National League for Opposing Suffrage, Wimbledon Branch*

Other MPS, POLICEMEN, SUFFRAGETTES, PRISON GUARDS, PRISON DOCTOR, MEMBERS OF THE PUBLIC

Note on the Text

In the final section of the play, the words 'one hundred years ago' refer to the centenary of the Representation of the People Act in 1918, as the play was first performed in 2018. Feel free to adjust the number of years according to when you are performing.

11 May 1909. We are in the Wimbledon Lecture Hall.

As the audience enters, they are treated as if they are members of the Wimbledon Women's Social and Political Union (WSPU) who have come to the lecture hall for today's speech. They are offered tea and cake.

As far as possible the space is decorated with the colours of the suffragette movement: white, purple and green. Historically on this day they filled the lecture hall with 'fragrant flowers'.

EDITH *talks to the audience. She is wearing purple, white and green.*

EDITH. I don't know about you, but I came for the cake.

I had no idea what this was all about – I was walking past the Lecture Hall on my way home, minding my own business, when this woman starts booming at me –

BERTHA. I say – chip chop, you're just in time!

EDITH. I beg your pardon?

BERTHA. You *are* here for the cause? You're wearing the colours.

EDITH. Am I?

BERTHA. Purple, white and green? Hurry in, dear, before the cake is entirely eaten.

EDITH (*to the audience*). You see it's one of my sternest principles: never, ever, pass up the opportunity for cake.

The original plan was to stuff a slice in my mouth and dash off. Then, when I got inside, I realised what it was: a suffragette meeting.

I'd seen them on the Common on Sunday afternoons. Skinny women freezing their bony bottoms off, banging on about women's lib. I did not think women needed the vote. If possible, I did not think at all. I had a husband to do that for me, while I focused on the garden.

She looks at the flowers around the room.

I say, what lovely foliage.

She takes a slice of cake, brings it toward her mouth –

BERTHA. First time, is it?

EDITH. Yes.

BERTHA. Bertha Lorsignol, Honorary Secretary of the Wimbledon Women's Social and Political Union. Welcome indeed. Mrs Montgomery Martin, will you find our new friend a place?

BEATRICE *approaches*.

BEATRICE. Hello there! I say! Have you come from one of the others? Oh, how marvellous! Let me see, the London Society for Women's Suffrage, the Liberal Women's Suffrage Society, or the Central Committee for Women's Suffrage?

EDITH. Yes – that one.

BEATRICE. You'll love it here. Honestly, she's absolutely glorious.

EDITH. She – ?

BERTHA (*raising her voice*). Ladies! Ladies. Mrs Lamartine Yates will be here shortly. For those who recently joined our ranks, Mrs Lamartine Yates sacrificed herself for the cause and was sent to Holloway Prison, where her sufferings were very great. And we are honoured today to be joined by two of her fellow prisoners, martyrs to the cause and guests of honour: Miss Emily Davison and Lady –

CONSTANCE *touches her on the arm slightly*.

Miss Constance Lytton.

EMILY *and* CONSTANCE *step forward*.

For these two inspirational women, the cause is their offspring, they love it like they would love their own child.

CONSTANCE. Under a government which imprisons anyone unjustly, the true place, for a just man or woman, is also a prison. As my friend here says –

EMILY. Rebellion against tyranny is obedience to God.

Wild applause. BERTHA *motions for them to join the audience.*

EDITH. I was beginning to wish I'd never come. These women are mad. No wonder nobody wants to marry them.

But then I saw her.

ROSE *cycles in.*

EDITH *holds her hand up for a moment and* ROSE *pauses.*

Alright, I know she probably didn't *actually* cycle straight into the room. She can't have. But that's what I remember.

Rose Lamartine Yates cycled into the Wimbledon Lecture Hall and changed my life forever.

ROSE *reaches her destination and hops off the bicycle.*

BERTHA (*in rapture*). Mrs Lamartine Yates!

BERTHA *starts clapping and soon the sounds of tumultuous applause and cheering fill the hall as a room full of women leaps to its feet. Perhaps the audience can be encouraged to join in.*

ROSE *is utterly calm and collected. She takes out some notes, and smiles graciously around at the audience.*

ROSE. Thank you! My dear friends and colleagues, how I have missed you!

They go quiet.

Shall we live the faith that is in us, fearing nothing, fearing no one, or shall we stand by when the light leads to suffering and to scorn? For weeks the thought haunted me. When my child grows up and asks 'What did you do, Mother, in the days of the women's agitation?' can I say 'Nothing?'

EDITH (*munching away on cake*). At first I didn't pay much attention. She went on a march, got arrested, it was all so silly.

Then she started talking about the police.

ROSE. They treated us with a degree of brutality I could never have believed without experiencing it. Blows on the breast, well aimed from clenched fists, thumbs pressed on the throat, and finally we were picked up, like a sack of corn, and flung on the steps of Caxton Hall.

EDITH. Now Gervase and I had always said these women deserved whatever they got, but they were only walking. And she didn't sound like a lunatic, she sounded like... a lawyer. Yes, that's it, she sounded like a *man*.

ROSE. In Holloway Prison, four of us were put in an intensely cold reception cell containing only one stool, and for food we were given a little lukewarm greasy cocoa in a filthy tin. At eleven o'clock in the night, I was stripped, weighed, and made to take a bath in public view.

The high walls were grey, the windows were grey, here all was grey, and the greyness of the surroundings crept into my very soul and made me doubt at times whether this cause of womanhood was worth such mental and physical suffering. The pain of hunger, the pain of sleeplessness and cold. Solitary confinement for twenty-three hours out of the twenty-four is like mental chloroform. The stagnation, the isolation, the system of depression, the intense inanity of the routine. But it *is* worth it. After all, what is a month's suffering, however acute, compared with the degradation inflicted on womanhood all over the world? Shall I flinch, knowing my pain is to uplift women? Never. I shall bear it all, proudly, gladly, and prove my faith.

The sound of clapping. ROSE *smiles and steps away.*

EDITH. She talked for a long time – I don't remember it all.

Then everyone started to leave, but I seemed unaccountably rooted to the spot.

EDITH *looks at the half-eaten piece of cake in her hand.*

She feels a bit sick.

She gives the cake to an audience member. She's struggling with an intense emotion that she doesn't understand.

ROSE *approaches. She is bright, smiley, efficient.*

ROSE. Is there something you need? Only I'm afraid Mrs Lorsignol ought to lock up.

EDITH. What about your husband?

ROSE. Tom? He couldn't come tonight, he's working.

EDITH. But he let you? Go to gaol?

ROSE. Oh, I see. Well, not *let* me exactly – it was my birthday present. We went to a speech by Mrs Pankhurst at the baths, and on the way home he happened to ask what I'd like for my birthday, and I said, 'A month in gaol, please.' So that was that.

EDITH. You left your baby.

ROSE. Yes. I did.

I'm sorry, we haven't met – I'm Rose – ?

EDITH. You shouldn't have done it. I think it's disgusting.

ROSE. And yet, here you are.

A beat.

EDITH. I… I don't know why I…

ROSE. It's alright. I remember my first time too, realising that things have to change. It's horrible.

EDITH. What you're doing here is a disgrace.

ROSE. Yes. But not doing it is worse.

ROSE *puts her hat on, picks up the bicycle.*

See you next week.

EDITH. I'm not coming back!

But ROSE *has gone.*

I walked straight home, but when I got there, I kept walking. I walked and walked, up and down the Ridgway. I was filled with a kind of fury – these women are unspeakable.

Anyway, a week later, I went back, just to make sure.

BERTHA. Ladies! Welcome! Please take your seats.

ROSE *steps forward for another speech.*

ROSE. Why are women barred from working in the professions? Why are women paid less than men for the same work? Why must we wear our hair up, and long skirts? How is it that a woman has no remedy to enforce justice? The answer comes: she has no voice in the choice of lawmakers. She is dumb.

The sound of applause.

EDITH. I had never heard a woman speak like this – as if she knew everything. It was surely only a matter of time before she'd tell us how to walk on water.

ROSE. Hello, again.

EDITH. How do you do that? Know what to say?

ROSE. I studied law, but women are not allowed to practise. So I have time on my hands.

EDITH. But the housework...?

ROSE. Well, we're lucky, I suppose, we have servants at Dorset Hall. And long ago I decided there were more useful ways I could fill my time than polishing the silverware. I am needed, you see. We all are. We must speak up, on behalf of the women who cannot.

EDITH. What if they don't want you to? They might be perfectly happy as they are.

ROSE. It is common for the captive to fall in love with captivity – and indeed the captor. But that's because they have forgotten the taste of freedom.

TOM *approaches.*

This is my husband. Tom, meet Mrs – ?

EDITH. Begbie. Edith.

TOM. How do you do? It was wonderful, Rose. One of my favourites! But I promised Nanny we'd be home on time tonight.

ROSE. See you next week, Mrs Begbie. It's always lovely to meet new members.

EDITH. I'm *not* a...

But they have gone. CONSTANCE *is there.*

CONSTANCE. It's hard, isn't it?

EDITH. Excuse me?

CONSTANCE. Waking up. To admit you've been having a damned long sleep, all this time. So much waste.

EDITH (*to the audience*). She actually said that – 'damned!'

CONSTANCE. I once saw some men try to capture a sheep that had escaped on its way to the slaughterhouse. They were useless, running about shouting like idiots. Around them a crowd of men, jeering and laughing.

That was the moment I woke up. Women are like that sheep. Running around in front of a group of men, being mocked, on our way to death.

EDITH. I'm not, I'm not *mocked* by anyone. I'm Mrs Edith Begbie, and I'm quite alright.

CONSTANCE. Well. I'm Constance, and I'm not alright in the least. It was nice to meet you, Mrs Begbie.

She starts to go.

EDITH. Goodnight, Lady Bulwer Lytton.

CONSTANCE *stops, turns back and looks at her, smiling a little.*

(*To the audience.*) I mean, it's one thing to fight for a cause, but to pretend one's father wasn't the Viceroy of India? I recognised her the moment I saw her.

CONSTANCE. You're going to be fabulous.

She goes, leaving EDITH *slightly stunned. And also, though she doesn't want to admit it, thrilled.*

EDITH. That night I told Gervase I was going to join the WI. He thought it was an excellent idea. I started to attend their meetings every week. I still didn't know how I felt about it, I just found myself going. To be in the presence of such certainty.

BERTHA *comes forward.*

BERTHA. Mrs Begbie, dear? Can you give out some leaflets?

She thrusts a handful of leaflets at EDITH.

EDITH. A march with a drum and fife band?

BERTHA. We meet at Victoria Crescent, march down the Broadway to Dorset Hall. Tea with Mrs Lamartine Yates. It will be tremendously arousing – our cries of jubilation will fill the streets of Wimbledon! This Saturday, at four p.m.

EDITH. Unfortunately I have a prior engagement.

BERTHA. Too busy for the cause, eh? Pity!

EDITH (*to the audience*). Coming to the talks was one thing. But a marching band of women? It seemed indecent. Imagine if someone recognised me?

I hurried home, full of sudden affection for Gervase. And when I got in, there he was, all cuddly and newspapery and everything you could ever want in a husband.

GERVASE *is there, reading the newspaper.*

GERVASE. You're home early.

EDITH. Darling, I missed you.

GERVASE. I say, it's the funniest thing – the women's movement has come to Wimbledon! Article here in *Punch* – look! There's a suffragette living in Dorset Hall, who went to prison – utterly abandoned her baby.

EDITH *looks at the newspaper.*

Can you imagine? Babies left crying alone, because women want the vote!

EDITH. Is it such a bad thing, Gervase, for women to have a vote?

GERVASE. Yes, it's silly, darling, I mean – *why*?

EDITH. I don't know, really. If you can vote, why not me?

GERVASE. Darling girl, I vote for us both. I promise. I always think of you, and what is best for *us*.

Are you very tired? You look a little off.

EDITH. I've got to go out on Saturday afternoon.

GERVASE. You haven't! I was going to ask Mother round for tea.

EDITH. Something with the WI.

GERVASE. Just me and old Tibs, again, I suppose.

EDITH (*to the audience*). Tibs was our cat. (*To* GERVASE.) I'll leave you a nice pie for lunch.

GERVASE. Well, if you have to go, there it is.

EDITH (*to the audience*). When the day came, I was trembling with nerves. I dressed in white so Gervase wouldn't think anything of it, but hid something purple under my petticoat – I never did anything like this in my life! I thought there would be at most twenty of us, wandering about.

But when I arrived, I couldn't believe my eyes. There were *four thousand* women.

We are suddenly deafened by the sound of the drum and fife marching band playing 'La Marseillaise'.

BERTHA *holds a placard reading 'VOTES FOR WOMEN', and* BEATRICE *is handing out WSPU sashes and placards to the audience, which say things like 'DEEDS NOT WORDS' or 'GIVE ME LIBERTY OR GIVE ME DEATH' and the Wimbledon WSPU banner.*

ROSE (*on a megaphone*). We ask for no privilege, no favour, we ask for fair play, for equal responsibility, and equal consideration. We have asked for forty years in vain! Our honour is at stake. Shall we submit, or shall we dare to be free? We shall dare, and our sons shall honour us!

EMILY. We shall never fail! We shall never falter! We shall never repent!

EDITH. Everywhere people with flags, cheering. Housemaids in upstairs rooms flinging open the windows and waving their handkerchiefs. All the way down the Broadway we marched, like a female army. They loved us!

At Dorset Hall a few of the organisers were arranging themselves for a photograph.

The company poses for a group photo.

BERTHA. Everyone face this way! Mrs Montgomery Martin? Miss Davison, your face is hidden –

CONSTANCE. Mrs Begbie, don't you want to be in the photograph?

EDITH. Me?

ROSE. Yes – come and join us!

They beckon her in. She is thrilled.

She joins them and there is a photo click and a flash.

A sudden clap of thunder and the sound of heavy rain.

BERTHA. Oh, ladies, I *said* it would rain!

ROSE. Come into the hall, everyone!

EDITH. We may have been an army, but one doesn't like to mess up one's hair.

We stayed at Dorset Hall until the evening. Talking and drinking tea and making plans. I ate four slices of cake.

As I walked home, I saw something painted on the gates at Dorset Hall. It hadn't been there when we arrived, I'm sure of it. It said 'Get back in the kitchen.'

And then another one that just said 'DIE'.

A beat.

A week later I signed the membership pledge on a small card.

BERTHA *hands* EDITH *a membership card.*

'I endorse the objectives of the Women's Social and Political Union.'

BEATRICE (*hugging her*). You're one of us, now.

EDITH. And so I became a suffragette.

REVEREND GODWIN *steps forward.*

REV GODWIN. From the Reverend G. H. Godwin, to the Editor of the *Wimbledon Borough News*, April the thirtieth, 1910.

'Sir.

Once upon a time, Church Lane was a pretty place. But the back gate of Dorset Hall has been turned into an advertisement site. A band turned up on a Saturday at four p.m., playing what was supposed to be the 'Marseillaise', with twenty-four ladies perspiring freely, five policemen, thirty-seven nursemaids, and about one hundred children.

I can only conclude, that as far as Merton is concerned, these women have ensured they will not get the vote this generation.'

EDITH. Don't you mind? They're so awful to you.

ROSE. Because they know they're losing! We are nearly there.

EDITH (*to the audience*). The year was nineteen hundred and ten. We were not nearly there. But I'm glad we didn't know that, then.

My first militant act was graffiti. We chalked pavements on the Broadway!

ROSE. We use white, purple and green chalk. And we'll stay together, for safety.

EDITH. But – people might see us?

ROSE. That's rather the point. It often attracts a large crowd.

EDITH. What are we writing?

ROSE. 'Votes for women. Speech on the Common, Sunday, two p.m.'

BERTHA *hands* EDITH *a piece of chalk. She pauses, uncertain.*

EDITH. Is this allowed?

ROSE. No.

EDITH. I never broke a rule in my life.

ROSE. You've never had a say in what the rules *are*.

EDITH *takes a big breath, kneels down and starts to chalk on the floor.* BEATRICE, BERTHA *and* ROSE *all join her.*

WOMAN. Here. What you doing? Are you one of them suffragettes?

BERTHA. We certainly are, madam.

BEATRICE. Should you like to join us on Sunday?

WOMAN. Might do. Might not.

BEATRICE. We hope to see you there!

The WOMAN *goes.*

EDITH. We chalked those pavements for two hours, up and down the centre of Wimbledon. The chalk broke frequently, and my back ached, and occasionally people took objection –

A MAN *walks up, deliberately rubs out the words with his feet.*

MAN. Never gonna happen.

He walks away.

BERTHA. How rude!

She writes the word again.

EDITH. But mostly it was exhilarating.

I began to sell the newsletter every Thursday, standing outside the station.

ROSE. Don't stand on the pavement – you might get arrested for obstruction. Stand in the road, but watch out for traffic.

EDITH *raises a newsletter above her head.*

EDITH. Votes for women! Only one penny.

Various people approach her and ROSE.

CHILD. 'Scuse me, miss, d'you wish you were a man?

EDITH. You should be in school.

MAN (*buying the paper*). Good luck, loves!

EDITH. Thank you.

YOUNG MAN. Look here, miss. If you get the vote, what are you going to do for us?

ROSE. We'll look after ourselves, I expect. Just like those who have a vote already.

YOUNG MAN. Here.

He motions for EDITH *to hand him a newsletter.* EDITH *does so and holds out her hand for the money. The* YOUNG MAN *rips it up in front of her, spits on the ground, and then goes.*

EDITH. Hey – that cost a penny!

One day, Lady Lytton joined us.

CONSTANCE *stands a little way away from them, newsletter in hand.*

CONSTANCE. Votes for women! Only a penny.

BEATRICE (*to* EDITH). Can you believe it? She's come all the way from Hertfordshire, just for us!

EDITH. I don't suppose she has much else to do with her time.

WOMAN (*to* CONSTANCE). 'Ere. I know you. You're one of them.

CONSTANCE. I am a proud member of the WSPU –

WOMAN. No, no, no, I seen your picture. You're one of them *society* women. What you doing here, telling us what to think, how would you know?

BEATRICE. Lady Lytton has spent time in prison, madam. She has suffered for the cause.

WOMAN. Oh yeah? Hard was it? Being a *lady*, in prison?

CONSTANCE. I'd like to think I was treated no differently because of my / name –

WOMAN. Right! Yeah, sure you'd like to think that. Cos I'm sure they treated you exactly the same as they would me!

The WOMAN *laughs and goes.* CONSTANCE *looks upset.*

GERVASE *approaches*. EDITH *is walking towards* CONSTANCE –

CONSTANCE. It's alright, she's telling the truth. You all think the same, I'm sure.

GERVASE. Edith?

EDITH *freezes, horrified*.

What on earth are you doing?

EDITH. Gervase...

ROSE *swoops in*.

ROSE. You must be Mr Begbie?

GERVASE. Yes, I am. Whatever is going on here?

ROSE. Mrs Lamartine Yates, of Dorset Hall, what a pleasure to meet you. Your charming wife has been good enough to support our cause today, when she came across our shop. Should you like to join us later for tea?

GERVASE. Well... no, I don't think so –

ROSE. I expect she's relieved you have arrived, and can walk her home. Goodbye, Mrs Begbie, it was a pleasure to meet you.

EDITH *and* GERVASE *walk away together.*

GERVASE. I say, isn't that the woman from *Punch*?! Just roped you in, did they?

EDITH. Yes.

GERVASE. Bad luck, old thing! What's for dinner?

EDITH (*to the audience*). He might have understood, if I had told him then, but I couldn't do it. I was brave enough to be spat at on the street, but not to tell my husband that I wanted the vote.

Weeks went by, and he must have thought that I was really very interested in long walks.

ROSE *comes forward, with her bicycle*.

ROSE. Ladies, good morning! I have just attended a very interesting meeting at Caxton Hall about the Census. I brought Miss Davison back with me, from the head offices of the WSPU.

EMILY *comes forward.*

EMILY. On the night of the Census, each house will be visited by an officer. The WSPU has made a decision: if women do not count, we shall not be counted.

BERTHA. Quite right!

EMILY. Women that are head of the household should write across their form: 'No votes for women: no information from women.' We shall strike out where it hurts them the most: in the heart of their administration systems!

ROSE. Miss Davison is going to take an even more drastic action on our behalf.

EMILY. On the night itself, I shall hide in the Houses of Parliament.

BEATRICE. Oh, you won't! I say, that's glorious!

BERTHA. Where will you hide?

EMILY. In a cupboard. I noticed it once during a protest, I thought it was about the right size to accommodate me for the night, so there I shall remain, eating bananas.

EDITH. But – won't you be arrested?

EMILY. Of course. I want to give my address as 'the Houses of Parliament'.

EDITH. But surely you – won't you...

She trails off, embarrassed.

ROSE (*gently*). What?

EDITH. Be terribly afraid...

EMILY. I don't know. Perhaps one day I shall find the limit of what I am prepared to do. But I haven't found it yet. Good luck, everyone!

EMILY *goes.*

ROSE. Are you alright?

EDITH. I don't think I can take part. I'm not the householder, that's Gervase.

ROSE. Then you must not be at home. If you are not there, you cannot be counted.

It's time to tell him, my dear.

EDITH *turns away, she draws a big breath.*

EDITH. Gervase.

GERVASE. Hello, old thing!

EDITH. There's something I've not been telling you, which explains why I've been a bit – well, absent, I suppose – these last few weeks –

GERVASE. Darling. I know.

EDITH. You do?

GERVASE. I worked it all out – dear Edith. It's marvellous!

EDITH. Really?

GERVASE. Of course!

EDITH. I'm so relieved! – I thought you might – I don't know, I thought you might disapprove.

GERVASE. Nonsense, it's what we both wanted, of course. How are you feeling? Perhaps you should stop all these long walks, you know.

A beat.

EDITH. Gervase, I'm not expecting a child.

I'm a suffragette.

GERVASE *stares at her.*

(*To the audience.*) He went as white as my dress. I was genuinely concerned about his blood pressure.

GERVASE. It's alright. I just – it's rather a... No little Begbie, then? On its way?

EDITH. No.

GERVASE. Just you. Wearing a sash.

EDITH. Sort of, yes.

GERVASE. Whatever will they think at the bank?

EDITH. I'm sorry to say, Gervase, I couldn't give two hoots.

GERVASE. Good God, I'll have to tell Mother. It could be the end for her, you know.

EDITH. For goodness' sake, I haven't contracted a contagious disease! I've just developed an opinion.

GERVASE. But – *why*? Why should you want to ruin everything?

He goes.

EDITH (*to* ROSE). He's gone away for a few days to stay with his mother.

ROSE. He'll be back.

EDITH. I expect so...

ROSE. Here.

She hands EDITH *a blanket.*

Wimbledon Common, at night.

EDITH. The Census was held on a Sunday night. There were about fifteen of us on Wimbledon Common. Three brought caravans, and drove them down the path. We had our boycott posters, of course, and we handed out leaflets until it got too dark. It was very, very cold.

What happens if we're caught?

ROSE. Officially, a five-pound fine, or a month in gaol.

EDITH. I'm... not ready. For gaol.

ROSE. If you need it, I can pay your fine. But I don't think they want the publicity.

CONSTANCE. They'd rather pretend our boycott isn't happening.

Enter BERTHA *and* BEATRICE.

BERTHA. Hulloo! Brave Boudicas!

BEATRICE. We're here!

BERTHA. I bring / cocoa!

BEATRICE. Mrs Lorsignol's got cocoa!

They start to hand around mugs of cocoa. They huddle together.

Isn't it super, to think of women all across the country doing this very same thing – camping out on floors and in shops.

BERTHA. Apparently there's a tremendously vigorous boycott in Plymouth.

BEATRICE. They can't throw us all in prison! They won't know what on earth to do.

EDITH. Would you go to prison again, Mrs Lamartine Yates?

ROSE. I promised Tom I wouldn't – Paul would notice my absence more now he's older. But if I asked – really asked – he's very good.

BERTHA. *Very* good.

ROSE (*to* EDITH). Mr Lorsignol is not so keen.

BERTHA. He says I've become mannish.

BEATRICE. Jessie Wheatley's husband tried to have her declared insane.

EDITH. Really?

ROSE. You'll be alright. Your Gervase is a good sort. He'll come round.

BEATRICE. And it will be worth it when we win.

EDITH. Do you honestly think we will?

BEATRICE. Absolutely!

BERTHA. Any day now the conciliation bill will be passed.

EDITH. But how can we know? Are we achieving anything, really?

ROSE. The wheel of destiny is suspended in eternity and depends for its onward movement on the proper distribution of the driving forces – the forces moving it should be man and woman.

A beat. BERTHA *is nodding solemnly,* EDITH *is looking at* ROSE *in disbelief.*

EDITH. How do you come up with these things off the top of your head? It's the most I can do to remember to wear a hat.

They burst out laughing.

(*To the audience.*) If I could only choose what to remember and what to forget, this night would occupy all the memories in my brain. I watched the sunrise on Wimbledon Common with Bertha Lorsignol, Rose Lamartine Yates, Beatrice Montgomery Martin, Constance Lytton, and a host of other women whose names I don't remember – but they were there, and they were important. We believed it was only a matter of time before people listened to us. I still thought, then, that asking nicely would work.

It's taken me a long time to understand that they were afraid of us.

They were afraid of what we would think, of whom we would elect. They were afraid it might not be them. So the conciliation bill proposed the vote only for women that owned a business or a house.

Not me, for instance.

ROSE. I know, I know. But it's a start. Mrs Pankhurst is organising a delegation of three hundred women to go to Parliament and be there to celebrate.

EDITH. Are you going?

ROSE. The Wimbledon branch has been offered three places in the delegation – but I can't go, Paul and Tom are both in bed with colds. It means we have a space free.

They all look at EDITH.

BERTHA. Mrs Begbie?

BEATRICE. Do come, Edith!

EDITH. I don't think – really, I –

ROSE. You'll be a part of history.

EDITH. But – Gervase has only just come home.

ROSE. Yes – it's so hard, isn't it?

ROSE backs away.

EDITH. Gervase? Do you mind me going?

GERVASE. Do you really want to know?

EDITH. I honestly think this will be the end of it. My last outing, as it were.

GERVASE. Don't dress it up, Edith. If you're going to go, go. If not, stay at home with me and Tibs. But don't pretend you'll wait for my permission.

A beat.

EDITH. I'll see you later.

She moves away. After she is out of hearing –

GERVASE. Be careful.

The sounds of a debate in the House of Commons. Speakers pop up from all around the space –

McLAREN. Walter McLaren, Member for Crewe. In what have women failed? What duty have you ever put upon women in which they have not succeeded? I am asking for women's suffrage as a man, because I think it will be the greatest reform we have ever had.

BUTCHER. Samuel Butcher, Member for Cambridge. The individual emotion of women is pretty dangerous. The collective emotion of women got up on this scale is a thing of which we have had no experience as yet in the world. I would therefore urge on the House they should not take this tremendous gamble in imperial affairs.

CHURCHILL. Winston Churchill, Secretary of State for Home Affairs. I do not believe that the great mass of women want the vote. And I am not in the least convinced that the male electorate of the country is in favour of making the change.

RANDOM MP 1. The argument that women do not want the vote is not relevant here. Even if they did want it, they should not have it.

RANDOM MP 2. I believe there are some here who look forward to a time when they see a woman in the Speaker's Chair!

Loud laughter.

Or perhaps a Prime Minister whose wife is the Leader of the Opposition!

More guffawing.

It seems absurd, but this is the potential consequence.

EDITH. We met at Caxton Hall – about three hundred of us, crammed into the hall with our banners.

EDITH *is there with* BEATRICE *and* BERTHA.

BEATRICE. This is it! Golly!

EDITH. I can't wait to go home to my husband and tell him it's all over.

BEATRICE (*handing* EDITH *a banner*). Oh, look! There she is!

EDITH. Standing on the platform, Christabel Pankhurst. In my memory she is tall, and surrounded by a bright white light, which can't be true. Above her the phrase 'Deeds Not Words' soared like a caption to a divine cartoon.

We were breathless foot soldiers waiting for the announcement that we had won the war.

PANKHURST *holds up her hand for silence.*

PANKHURST. I have just received a message that the Prime Minister intends to dissolve Parliament. We have waited, and trusted, and waited again, but we have been betrayed. The conciliation bill is dead.

A shout of fury through the crowd.

We shall march to Parliament Square in groups of twelve. Maintain your dignity, ladies, and hold your banners high. We shall go to Mr Asquith, and insist on being heard. We shall wait there, and refuse to move, until we are.

EDITH. We filed down the streets. I didn't know what to expect, I was used to people cheering us in Wimbledon. But something was wrong from the beginning. We were surrounded by police and onlookers – all men. There were no waving women, no friendly housemaids in the upstairs windows. A sea of brown caps, and flat, angry faces. All around us, moving in, closer and closer.

They don't look very welcoming.

BERTHA. They're not the usual police – they're from the East End, more used to dealing with drunks than suffragettes.

EDITH. Where are the normal police?

BERTHA. Cornwall. There's a miners' strike.

They look around them fearfully. The noise grows menacing.

BEATRICE. Goodness.

BERTHA. Let's stay together, dears.

They hold hands and face the crowd.

Normally Mr Churchill issues an order for the police to arrest us, pretty quick. So we won't get hurt, just charged. It might be a bit rough, but it won't last long.

EDITH. What happens if Mr Churchill doesn't issue the order?

BERTHA. I don't know.

A POLICEMAN *suddenly pushes* EDITH *away from* BEATRICE.

POLICEMAN. This way, madam.

BERTHA. Oh – Mrs Begbie – Mrs Begbie! Young man – how dare you push her?

The POLICEMAN *turns back on* BERTHA. EDITH *steps in to intervene –*

EDITH. It's alright, he's just ignorant.

The POLICEMAN *punches her in the stomach. Then he grabs her by the hair, with* BERTHA *shouting –*

BERTHA. This is illegal – you brute – take your hands off her at once! Who do you think you are?

The POLICEMAN *slaps* BERTHA, *then turns back to* EDITH.

POLICEMAN. Haven't you heard? We can do whatever we like today.

He goes.

EDITH. We couldn't get away. All around us I could hear women crying and shouting for help. It lasted six hours. Until at last, the police arrested some of us, and went away, and it was quiet.

BEATRICE *helps* EDITH *to her feet.*

BEATRICE. It's over.

It's alright. You're alright.

EDITH. Where's Mrs Lorsignol?

BEATRICE. I don't know, I lost sight of her –

EDITH. She was hurt –

BEATRICE. They're letting us go now. We need to go / back to the –

EDITH. Where does Mr Churchill live?

BEATRICE. Pimlico.

EDITH *walks off, staggering slightly.*

Mrs Begbie?

EDITH. Are you coming?

A beat. Then BEATRICE *joins her.*

They walk together, all around the space, weaving through the audience.

The streets were quiet now. It was barely a mile's walk.

They both pick up large stones.

He had a nice house, Mr Churchill. Tall white pillars. Lovely big windows.

EDITH *and* BEATRICE *throw their stones at the windows. The sound of smashing glass. They stand still, waiting for their arrest.*

We were arrested straight away this time. Breaking the law was a considerably more pleasant experience than peaceful protest.

ROSE. I say, Mrs Begbie! Churchill's windows? Golly. Well done, you!

EDITH. If he can break the spirits and bodies of women, I can break his windows.

ROSE. Tom is going to represent you in court. But you'll get a prison sentence, I'm afraid.

EDITH. I don't care. Will you tell Gervase?

ROSE. Yes.

EDITH *is dragged away, and as she goes –*

Edith? Keep your spirits up! Listen for us.

The space goes dark. EDITH *huddles on a bed in a bare cell, it is very cold.*

EDITH. Mrs Lamartine Yates had been right about solitary confinement. I traced the spaces between the bricks of my cell. I learnt the shape of the bars and their shadows. Sometimes I replayed the demonstration over and over again in my head.

I tried to remember that I was not alone. That I was one of all of us – all of you – in every home; for every child there is a mother and I was doing this for them.

A whisper from the cell next door.

EMILY. Mrs Begbie? It's Emily. Emily Davison.

EDITH. Hello...

EMILY. Have they hurt you?

EDITH. No. Not physically.

EMILY. Nor me. But I want them to. I'm going to force them to, I want blood on their hands.

EDITH. What are you going to do?

EMILY. Nothing. I'm not going to do anything at all, and that includes eating.

EDITH. A hunger strike?

EMILY. Yes.

EDITH. Shall I do it too?

EMILY. If you want to. Let's all do it. We'll just stop.

EDITH. I didn't think it would go on for long. I thought, we'll make our point for a few days, perhaps they'll even be embarrassed and let us out.

Then one morning I heard screams. They had started force-feeding.

It happened to me for seven days, so I do remember it, although I try not to.

I sit on the bed, waiting. I tell myself that I'm going to struggle, but when I see the people who are going to treat me, they look like nice ordinary people, and I don't want to make things hard for them. They look as awkward and upset by the whole business as I am.

They pin me to the chair and put a sheet across my body under my chin. The doctor says –

DOCTOR. You have one last chance: will you eat your food?

EDITH. No.

DOCTOR. You can have a wooden or a steel gag. The wooden one is better, softer on your teeth. You can choose, but you need to cooperate. Open your mouth.

EDITH *keeps her mouth clamped shut.*

Very well.

EDITH. From behind my head he forces my mouth open and places a steel gag inside. By turning a screw, the gag expands so that my jaws are forced apart. He pushes a rubber tube down my throat. It goes a long way – I can feel it scraping – I can't breathe – it surely has reached my stomach, but I can't tell them that, I can't say – this is agony, please stop, you are going to kill me. The sounds I make are not something I have ever heard before.

They pour liquid down the tube – I think it is milk and bread – the lumps are too big, everything is stuck. Then they pull the rubber tube back out and I vomit on the floor.

Is it worth it?

Am I doing anything at all? Will they thank me?

Or will I just die here, and be forgotten?

A pause.

We tried to keep our spirits up. We would whisper to each other, words of encouragement or prayers. We would not let them break us.

EMILY *is pacing up and down her cell, muttering to herself.*

EMILY. I'm going to smash the windows. I'm going to set myself on fire –

She starts to move chairs in front of the door to her cell.

EDITH (*hearing the noise*). Emily – what are you doing? Are you alright?

EMILY. I won't let them do it to me again. I won't let this happen.

GUARD (*banging on the door*). Davison! Open the door! Open up immediately.

EMILY. What are you going to do? What are you going to do to us next? We are political prisoners, we have rights! We are not criminals! Stop torturing us!

EDITH. They forced a fire-hose pipe through her cell window, and turned it on for fifteen minutes.

The sound of a hose pipe spurting water, loud and hard and freezing cold. EMILY *screams. She crouches on the floor as the water continues to flood her cell.*

EMILY. No surrender! No surrender!

Eventually the water stops, and EMILY *is left alone on the floor of her cell.*

No surrender.

EDITH. They took her away a few hours later, and force-fed her again.

EMILY *gets up slowly, and staggers off.*

Emily?

Emily?

The next day, we were allowed out for exercise.

BEATRICE *joins* EDITH *in the prison yard.*

Emily's gone.

BEATRICE. Apparently she threw herself off one of the interior balconies of the prison.

EDITH. What? She's not – is she – ?

BEATRICE. Her fall was broken by netting. She cracked two vertebrae and badly injured her head.

EDITH. At least they'll stop force-feeding her for a bit.

BEATRICE. No. They have already done it again.

Keep walking, dear. Try not to let them see you're upset.

EDITH. I think we're going to die here.

BEATRICE. They can't have that. The publicity would be too awful. They'll release Emily tomorrow.

EDITH. Perhaps we'll just go mad instead.

From far away, the sound of music. The company, all women in suffragette colours, stand together at the gates of the prison.

BEATRICE. Listen. It's them.

The suffragette women are singing 'The March of the Women' –

'Shout, shout, up with your song,
Cry with the wind, for the dawn is breaking – '

The singing rises.

EDITH *and* BEATRICE *stand together, holding hands perhaps.*

Remember: they *cannot let us die.*

A moment of peace.

After four months, I was released. I thought Gervase would be there at the gates; awfully cross, of course, but *there*.

ROSE, *holding a placard: 'TO ASK FREEDOM FOR WOMEN IS NOT A CRIME.'*

ROSE. Mrs Begbie! Well done! We're taking you to breakfast.

EDITH. Where's Gervase?

A beat.

ROSE. I went to your house. I asked if he would like to come and meet you.

EDITH. It's alright.

ROSE. Give him time.

EDITH. Where shall I go?

ROSE. Dorset Hall, of course. Mrs Montgomery Martin is there already, she was released earlier. You shall recover together, it'll be so jolly.

She takes her arm.

Wait till you see the hall – everyone's there!

EDITH. What about Emily?

ROSE. Come...

EDITH. I could hear the party as we walked down the road. The sound of china teacups seemed extraordinary.

ROSE. Here she is! Our brave soldier!

The sounds of clapping and cheering, whooping and whistling, goes on for ages. EDITH *is overwhelmed.*

Eventually it goes quiet.

Mrs Begbie was imprisoned for four months. She went on hunger strike and was forcibly fed. She has endured unimaginable pain and humiliation.

CONSTANCE. It is my great privilege to present Mrs Begbie with this medal in recognition of her courage.

CONSTANCE *presents* EDITH *with a Hunger Strike Medal. More clapping and cheering.*

ROSE. Mrs Begbie, we have thought of you without ceasing. Many of the women here have undergone a week of voluntary self-denial in solidarity.

EMILY *comes forward, she is walking stiffly, perhaps with a stick.*

EMILY. Ladies. We are here today to share our first meal together to show our love and admiration for this heroine. She will, from now on, always be a suffragette martyr in our eyes.

Tears are streaming down EDITH*'s face.* ROSE *helps her to sit down.*

ROSE. Rest, now, Edith. Get better.

EDITH *sits down, and closes her eyes.*

EDITH. It was nearly July, and the weather was warm. Dorset Hall had a large garden, with a hammock down at the shady end. We would sleep and read for the whole day, with little Paul playing on a rug at our feet.

One day, I had a visitor.

GERVASE *comes forward.*

A beat.

GERVASE. Hello, old thing.

EDITH. I wanted to be angry with him. But his jacket was inside out.

It's nice to see you.

GERVASE. You look... God...

EDITH. I'm better than I was.

How are you?

GERVASE. Oh, I'm fine. Mother comes round. Does the washing.

There's a problem, though. It's Tibs. He misses you.

EDITH. Tibs?

GERVASE. He can't really function without you, to be honest.

Tibs thinks, if a man loves his wife, he'd probably better want the things she wants, if at all possible. And Tibs found it hard to want the same things, but he's worked it out now, and feels like a bit of a fool. Because Tibs thinks that if a man's wife wants something so much she goes to prison for it... and gets treated horribly... then, really, the man ought to turn up and jolly well give them a black eye. He ought to admit that he thinks they're. Bastards. Utter bastards.

How *dare* they touch you?

EDITH. Darling, don't.

GERVASE. Tibs is very, very angry. With himself, and with them, and himself...

Edith?

EDITH. Yes?

GERVASE. When I say Tibs, I mean me.

EDITH. Yes, I realised that.

GERVASE. Please come home.

EDITH. We walked home together, and it was bliss to be walking down our dear old street, towards our dear old house.

GERVASE. Welcome home.

EDITH. Darling, wait. I'm going to carry on. I can't stop now. I'm sorry if that upsets you – and your mother and the bank and everyone else – but if I stop now it will all be for nothing. And if you don't like that, I shouldn't even stay a single night. I'm sorry, but there it is.

A beat.

GERVASE. You should come in here.

He walks off. She follows him.

EDITH. Please – don't brush this under the carpet –

She stops.

Good heavens. Whatever happened to the study?

GERVASE. I thought you'd need somewhere to work. Write your letters. Plan your next jumble sales, speeches, window-smashing...

EDITH. Gone was the tobacco smoke and the leather chair and the pile of newspapers. Instead flowers and a new table and walls painted green and purple – which looked dreadful, actually, but this didn't seem the time –

GERVASE. Do you like it?

Room of your own. So to speak.

EDITH. Gervase, have you been reading Mary Wollstonecraft?

GERVASE. Well, the synopsis. I got the gist.

EDITH. It's wonderful.

GERVASE. Good. Best get to work then. Sort these buggers out.

He goes.

EDITH. I got to work. I joined the committee, and took over the running of the shop.

In the four months since I had been away, new groups had begun to spring up all over South London.

MRS GLADSTONE. Mrs Gladstone Salome Ards, Chairman of the National League for Opposing Suffrage, Wimbledon Branch.

BERTHA. Can you believe it?

BEATRICE. They use *our* meeting rooms at Compton Hall!

MRS GLADSTONE. The trouble is that women do not understand finance, except in a purely local sense. We must have safety at home and abroad, the Empire relies upon it, and this is a dangerous slide towards socialism.

ROSE. Let's have a debate, Mrs Gladstone. Let us discuss these things in a civilised manner.

MRS GLADSTONE. A militant suffragette cannot be trusted to be *civilised*.

(*To the audience*.) Ladies and gentleman, you should know that this woman's husband, a *lawyer*, was recently arrested for attending a demonstration.

ROSE. He was released without charge.

MRS GLADSTONE. I don't know about you, but when I choose a solicitor, I prefer him not to have a criminal record.

EDITH. Will Tom lose all his clients?

ROSE. There aren't many left to lose.

EDITH. We wrote letters to newspapers, we spent every Sunday on the Common.

EMILY (*speaking on the Common*). The true militant suffragette is an epitome of the determination of women to possess their own souls. To lay down life for friends, that is glorious, selfless, inspiring! But to re-enact the tragedy of Calvary – the ultimate self-sacrifice – for generations unborn, that is the last and consummate sacrifice of the militant! She will not hesitate even unto the last.

Applause.

EDITH. But it didn't matter how well we spoke. How politely we asked. They only hated us more.

Once I got up in the dead of night and carved 'Votes for Women' in the turf of Wimbledon Golf Course.

BERTHA. I say! Mrs Begbie...

EDITH. I had to do it.

BERTHA. It's in all the papers.

EDITH. They don't care about half the population being mistreated, but they care about golf.

ROSE. Mrs Lorsignol has a point: if possible, I should like to continue to have the support of our friends who live here. It makes things easier.

EDITH. They sit back and watch while women are tortured. They are not our friends.

EMILY. She's right. We keep going. We never surrender.

ROSE. Alright. Such as?

BEATRICE. More windows.

EDITH. We could throw stones at passing cars with politicians in?

EMILY. Bombs in letterboxes.

They all gasp.

BEATRICE. Goodness.

BERTHA. No. Absolutely not.

EMILY. It's the only way –

BERTHA. Someone will get hurt –

EDITH. We're already hurting!

BERTHA. I can't do it. I won't do that.

EDITH. It's the / only –

BERTHA. I'm sorry. This is beyond my limits, my husband would –

It's not right, it's too far.

ROSE. Mrs Lorsignol –

BERTHA. I don't want to know about it. If you must continue, then by all means do, but make your plans without me. The less I know the better.

She starts to go.

ROSE. You could stay with me.

BERTHA *pauses*.

If he throws you out, you can stay with me.

BERTHA. And what about my children? When he gets custody, will you explain why to them, too? Because their mother put a *bomb* in a letterbox?

ROSE. But you're my – Bertha – you're the co-founder!

BERTHA. Not any more.

I'm sorry. I simply –

BERTHA *goes*.

EDITH. She was not the only one that left. But more joined.

And now we had the attention of the whole nation. We could not stop, even if we wanted to. Whether a suffragette would die in gaol had become a national question: an interesting debate for guests over dinner.

I went back to prison, but this time as a visitor.

CONSTANCE, *dressed in prison clothing, her hair cut short, fake glasses that have been broken.*

EDITH *looks at her.* CONSTANCE *is clearly ill. A moment.*

Oh, my –

CONSTANCE. How did you get in?

EDITH. I said I was your sister.

CONSTANCE. What did you call me – did you give me away – ?

EDITH. No. Mrs Lamartine Yates told me you've changed your name. You're called Jane now?

CONSTANCE. Wanted to see what it was like. Not being a lady in prison. Threw a stone at a window in front of a policeman. Got my answer.

EDITH. You don't look / well –

CONSTANCE. Jane Wharton is scum of the earth. It's as if I'm not there. Worse – I *am* there, and they wish I wasn't. They kneel on my chest while they feed me, and when I vomit the doctor hits me.

EDITH. Actually – ?

CONSTANCE. Not hard. Just enough to show how he feels. He said if I was sick again he'd feed me twice.

EDITH. You need to eat. Stop the hunger strike, ask to go to the infirmary.

CONSTANCE. I couldn't remember the rules – what did we say we'd do, can we choose the wooden over the steel gag, because I'm refusing to speak so they use the steel one, and I think my teeth are going to fall out –

EDITH. Lady Ly–

CONSTANCE. Shh!

EDITH. Jane – Jane, it doesn't matter, choose the wooden one if it hurts less.

CONSTANCE. Which did you choose?

EDITH. I – don't remember.

CONSTANCE. You see? You had more strength than me.

CONSTANCE starts to cry.

EDITH. Tell them who you are. Please.

CONSTANCE starts to unbutton her shirt, revealing an angry scar at the top of her chest.

What – what is that?

CONSTANCE. It's supposed to be a 'V'.

A PRISON GUARD looms.

PRISON GUARD. Stop that! It's indecent!

She does her shirt up again.

EDITH. Who did it this to you?

CONSTANCE. I did it myself. With a hat pin I found in the exercise yard.

I wanted to write 'Votes for Women' all the way down my body, but it wouldn't stop bleeding.

I couldn't even do that.

A bell rings.

PRISON GUARD. It's time.

CONSTANCE. Write to my mother for me?

EDITH. Of course.

CONSTANCE. Don't tell her I cried, for God's sake! Say – oh God, I don't know what to say –

EDITH (*taking her hands tightly*). I'll tell her, you're doing this for Jane Wharton.

Remember you are wanted, all women are wanted, for who they are, because they are women.

A beat.

CONSTANCE. I said you'd be fabulous.

EDITH. No surrender.

CONSTANCE. No. Yes. No surrender.

EDITH *turns back to the audience.*

EDITH. Everyone was talking about us, now, about what we might do next. Mrs Lamartine Yates continued to speak every Sunday on the Common, as usual.

TOM *hovers, anxiously.*

ROSE. Tom, it's fine.

TOM. There must be twenty thousand people out there.

ROSE. Good.

TOM. I called the police.

ROSE. Why? Do you think I can't manage?

TOM. You know they don't want you to be hurt.

EDITH. Wasn't my experience.

TOM. It's different here, Mrs Begbie, honestly. The superintendent came round for dinner last week. If anyone turns on you out there, Rose, you must have protection.

ROSE. They are only afraid because they think we are going to win.

She turns to the audience, stepping on a platform and raising her voice –

I wish to talk about the everyday struggles of women. The housewife of low to middle income –

A sudden loud sound like a foghorn. The sounds of booing. She carries on –

The housewife of low to middle income has no legal rights to her own children, even though she is their creator...

The booing is louder.

PERSON IN CROWD 1. What about the damage on the golf course?

PERSON IN CROWD 2. What about the window-smashing? D'you support violence?

ROSE. Broken glass may be repaired at a small cost; but the broken and ruined lives of women who have been mistreated, no money can repair.

MAN IN CROWD. You shouldn't be out here! Get back indoors!

ROSE. I have as much right as you to be here. You will not deny my right to speak.

MAN IN CROWD. If you were my wife, I'd poison yer food!

ROSE. If you were my husband, I'd eat it.

Laughter, applause, but also more booing – and the mood grows uglier. Something is thrown at ROSE *– rotten fruit? An egg? It hits her. Then more is thrown, and more.* ROSE *ducks.*

EDITH. They pressed closer and closer to the platform. I heard someone say 'stop them' and then as Mrs Lamartine Yates was knocked down, a cry went up – 'the women are down, kill them.'

TOM. We need to go!

EDITH *jumps up and helps take* ROSE *off the platform. They run around the space, to* EDITH*'s house. From outside, the sounds of jeering and booing mingle with police sirens.*

EDITH (*to the audience*). My house was the closest, so we ran there.

It's alright, I've locked the doors.

TOM. Good God, it's not a crowd, it's a mob. (*To* ROSE.) Are you hurt?

ROSE (*looking out of the window*). Poor bobbies – they're completely overstretched.

The sound of glass being smashed. They jump.

Oh, dear, Edith, that was one of your front windows I'm afraid.

The crowd roars outside.

EDITH. They hate us so much.

ROSE. They cannot stop us from speaking. They will not. That would be the worst – Edith, that would be the worst thing.

EDITH. They never will.

We were barricaded in my house for an hour, until the mob gave up and went away.

I think the coast's clear.

ROSE. We need to get home.

TOM. Rose –

ROSE. I've got another speech in my head – I need to write it down straight away. Are you coming?

TOM. Just – give me a minute?

ROSE *nods and goes.*

TOM *and* EDITH *are left alone.*

EDITH. What is it?

TOM. When she was a child she was constantly ill – she has a weak spine and chest. She had a breakdown, just before we were married. She got pleurisy when she went to prison last year. I'm not sure how much longer she can keep this up.

EDITH. She has you.

TOM. I'm sixty-five, Edith.

I won't be here for ever. I need you to help me to help her.

A beat.

EDITH. No.

TOM. You don't mind if she gets ill?

EDITH. I've just watched a crowd of violent men baying for blood outside my house. The whole country is ill.

You should walk her home.

TOM *goes.*

I knew that something was going to happen, something that would change it all. But when it did, it was still a shock.

TOM *comes forward with a telegram for* ROSE.

In June, Emily took a train to Epsom to attend the Derby. She carried two flags with the suffragette colours. On the final bend before the home straight, she ducked under the barriers and ran out in front of a horse.

ROSE. She's in the hospital. They'll need a lawyer.

TOM. We'll go together.

EDITH. Emily Davison took four days to die. Enough time for the newspapers to declare that she was a hateful lunatic, and for people to write letters to the hospital declaring they hoped she would die in agony. And it was enough time for Rose Lamartine Yates to decorate her bed with purple, white, and green.

ROSE. Mrs Begbie –

EDITH. You're back.

ROSE. Type this on headed paper. 'The public funeral of Miss Emily Wilding Davison will take place on Saturday next, June the fourteenth. The body will be brought up from Epsom in the morning, and escorted by a procession from Victoria to St George's Church in Bloomsbury.'

TOM. Rose – give her a minute.

ROSE *rolls out a map.*

ROSE. I've split the procession into Sections A to J. VIPs from the WSPU and Emily's friends making a guard of honour at the front. Hunger-strikers go in Section E; prisoners behind them. Everyone gathers at one p.m., we leave at two.

TOM. Rose – why don't we –

ROSE. Everyone dressed in black. Be prepared to take action, and be arrested. Otherwise don't even bother to come. Is that clear?

EDITH. Yes –

ROSE. She's the first. How many more? How many?

TOM (*very firm*). Not you, please. Sit down –

ROSE. We need to stress that she had a first-class degree – that she was conscientious and clever and not a mad hysterical woman. If they take this death from us then I cannot bear it – I shall set fire to the Houses of Parliament myself.

TOM. Rose! You are a pacifist. You would never deliberately harm a living creature. Not even a / goldfish –

ROSE. She didn't mean to do it. I don't know why she ran out onto the course, but she wasn't planning to die.

She always talked about not being heard. She said to me once that she felt she had been screaming for so long, that words weren't enough. She wanted to use her whole body.

How much longer? How much more screaming?

EDITH. She did not stop to rest, even for a day or two. I could have tried to stop her, but I didn't. I smashed windows, I committed wilful arson, I broke the law many times, but this was the worst thing I did. I encouraged her.

(*To* ROSE.) We have neglected our fundraising lately – we'll run out altogether soon. I was thinking about that garden party – how about when you return from the Leicester by election?

ROSE. Good idea.

TOM. No! Absolutely not.

A beat. They are surprised by his tone.

I have never forbidden anything, Rose, you know I support everything you do, but if you keep going at this rate –

ROSE. I feel absolutely / fine –

TOM. You will listen to me, Rose! For once, will you please respect what I have to say? Let Edith take this one. She could run the garden party, couldn't you?

They turn to EDITH.

EDITH. We both need to be there.

ROSE. You see?

TOM. A garden party doesn't just happen by itself! It's cooking, cleaning, preparing food for sixty –

EDITH. We desperately need more funds.

ROSE. Quite.

EDITH. Unless you have a better suggestion?

TOM *backs away in frustration.*

It was a hot day, and the garden at Dorset Hall was filled with people.

ROSE *is at her garden party, giving a speech.*

ROSE. How long shall we accept that we have no right to be in the place where decisions are made that decide our own futures, our own rights?

Emily Davison saw that this cannot continue. She did not want to die because she hated life. We, that knew her, knew her passions, that she loved to live. She would do anything for anyone. She gave everything for us. She wanted to die because of us. You, and me.

She was –

A pause.

TOM *wants to step in. He whispers – 'Rose'...*

She was my –

Friend, she was my –

Another pause. Then, a quiet instruction –

Tom.

She faints. He reaches her just in time to stop her hitting the floor.

EDITH *steps forward to help –*

EDITH. Rose!

TOM. Go away, please. You've done enough.

Shocked, EDITH *backs off.* TOM *carries* ROSE *gently away.*

EDITH. She did not die, that day. He took her and Paul to France, and stayed there for many months.

She had visitors, sometimes. I went, once.

But mostly they wanted to be alone.

Constance Lytton had a heart attack and two strokes. She returned to Knebworth to be looked after by her mother. She survived, just.

When the war broke out, we turned our shop into a soup kitchen. For a while, I was the steward, long hours cooking cheap meals for women and children whose husbands went off to war and never came home. Then when Gervase was wounded on the Somme, I had to stop. I didn't see them for a while.

Until a cold day in February 1918, when Gervase handed me the newspaper.

GERVASE, *limping heavily and awkwardly, with a crutch.*

GERVASE. Edith.

It's over. You've done it.

She stares at the front page. Then they look at each other. An understanding.

EDITH. I'll be back in a bit.

GERVASE *nods, smiles.*

She was sitting outside, as I had known she would be, with her bicycle propped against the bench.

ROSE *is there.*

They sit together.

I thought I would feel different.

ROSE. You can't really celebrate without champagne, that's the trouble.

EDITH. Lord, I haven't seen champagne for years. I don't suppose it exists any more.

ROSE. We didn't plan for victory, did we? We celebrated hunger strikes, and prison sentences, and all sorts of horrible things. We never planned what to do when we won.

EDITH. *Elector*. Good word.

ROSE. Still not all of us.

EDITH. No. But eight-point-four-million women is a very good start.

ROSE. How will they talk about us? Will they say we were heroines, like we told ourselves we were? Or lunatics? What if Churchill and all the rest of them were right, and we do turn out to be emotional half-witted imbeciles that vote for communism?

EDITH. I think lunacy must be equally distributed amongst the sexes. I mean, Gervase loves our cat more than any rational person ever could.

ROSE. How is he?

EDITH. Gervase? Oh, *super*, he just doesn't have a left leg.

Sorry.

ROSE. All wars are terrible.

EDITH. Are you better?

ROSE. Do you think me an awful shirker? Running off like that at the end?

EDITH. Of course not.

ROSE. I always wanted to do what was right, at any cost. But sometimes I couldn't see the right road. Fighting is so lonely. And then I cursed myself for being ridiculous. You have such faith.

EDITH. I didn't at first. I didn't have any thoughts at all. When I met you that first time, I only came in for the cake. But then I heard you speak, and it –

It was wonderful, what you did.

Thank you.

ROSE. Did you get it? The cake?

EDITH. Plenty.

ROSE. Good.

A beat.

EDITH. Gervase hates to be alone...

ROSE. Of course. I'm off to Victoria Crescent, in any case. It's February, but apparently we're having a meeting about this year's Christmas pudding.

EDITH *starts to go. She stops –*

EDITH. We did do it, you know. It was one hell of a battle, but we fought it, and we won.

ROSE. We shouldn't have had to.

She is crying. EDITH *impulsively flings her arms round her. They hold each other tightly for a moment. Then they part.*

Goodbye, Mrs Begbie.

EDITH. Goodbye, Mrs Lamartine Yates.

EDITH *turns back to the audience.*

ROSE *is joined by* BEATRICE, EMILY, CONSTANCE (*with a walking stick or using a wheelchair*), BERTHA, TOM, *and* GERVASE, *standing with his stick.*

One hundred years ago, some women won the right to vote.

TOM. One hundred and ten years ago, the Wimbledon branch of the Women's Social and Political Union began to hold meetings in rooms like this one.

GERVASE. They raised money and gave speeches and waved banners and they were ignored, abused and imprisoned.

EMILY. Some of them did things they shouldn't have.

BEATRICE. Some of them discovered they were not as nice as they had thought they were.

CONSTANCE. They regret what they did, they regret that they had to do it at all; and their regrets haunt the rooms like ghosts.

ROSE. So when you next walk into a hall like this one, with your voting slip in hand, listen for the whispers of the women that went before you.

EMILY. The women who sat in a prison cell thinking of all the women of the future, who will be allowed to mark a single cross in a box on a ballot paper.

BEATRICE. We want you to know that you count.

BERTHA. We want your opinions to be heard.

EDITH. We want you to find that the dawn will break, in the end.

The End.

www.nickhernbooks.co.uk

@nickhernbooks